Piano Solo

IT IS WELL

❧ 10 BELOVED HYMNS FOR MEMORIAL SERVICES ❧

ARRANGED BY JOHN PURIFOY

ISBN 978-1-4803-4078-7

HAL•LEONARD® CORPORATION

7777 W. BLUEMOUND RD. P.O. BOX 13819 MILWAUKEE, WI 53213

In Australia Contact:
Hal Leonard Australia Pty. Ltd.
4 Lentara Court
Cheltenham, Victoria, 3192 Australia
Email: ausadmin@halleonard.com.au

Visit Hal Leonard Online at
www.halleonard.com

FOREWORD

In the years my wife and I have played piano for church services and special events, some of the most meaningful and poignant moments have occurred during the memorial services of dear friends and family members—many of whom had favorite hymns that reflected their lives of faith. Although these settings may be used in general worship services throughout the year, I especially hope they will bring comfort as loved ones are remembered and celebrated.

John Purifoy

CONTENTS

ABIDE WITH ME

Words by HENRY F. LYTE
Music by WILLIAM H. MONK
Arranged by John Purifoy

Legato, with reverence

pedal harmonically

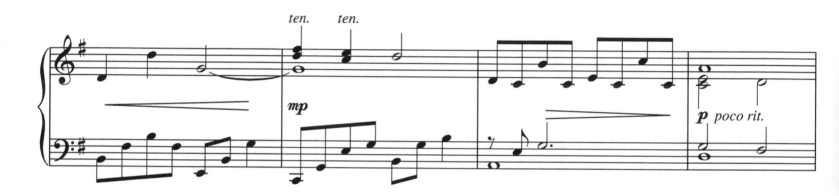

Slower, freely

AMAZING GRACE

Words by JOHN NEWTON
Traditional American Melody
Arranged by John Purifoy

With peaceful grace

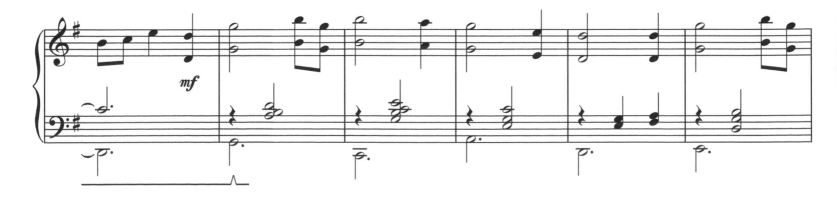

Slower

In loving memory of Susan Robins Purifoy

BE STILL, MY SOUL

Words by KATHARINA von SCHLEGEL
Music by JEAN SIBELIUS
Arranged by John Purifoy

Peacefully

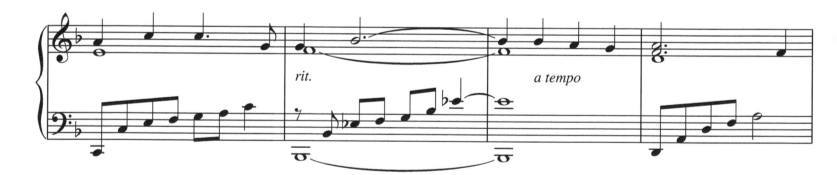

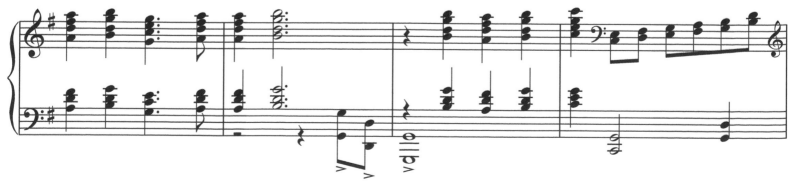

FOR ALL THE SAINTS

Words by WILLIAM W. HOW
Music by RALPH VAUGHAN WILLIAMS
Arranged by John Purifoy

Victoriously, with assurance

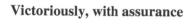

Stately

WHAT A FRIEND WE HAVE IN JESUS

Words by JOSEPH M. SCRIVEN
Music by CHARLES C. CONVERSE
Arranged by John Purifoy

Gently

pedal liberally for ethereal quality

HIS EYE IS ON THE SPARROW

Words by CIVILLA D. MARTIN
Music by CHARLES H. GABRIEL
Arranged by John Purifoy

Tenderly, with freedom

pedal harmonically

IN THE GARDEN

Words and Music by
C. AUSTIN MILES
Arranged by John Purifoy

Warmly, with freedom

mp

pedal harmonically

rall.

a tempo

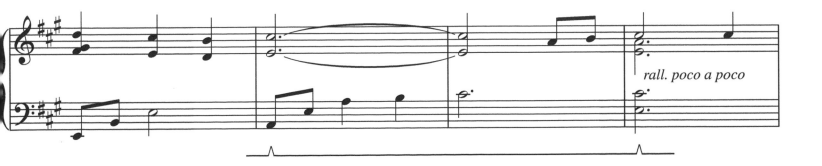

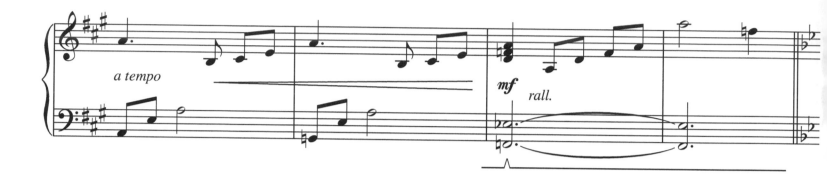

rall.   a tempo

mp   molto rit.

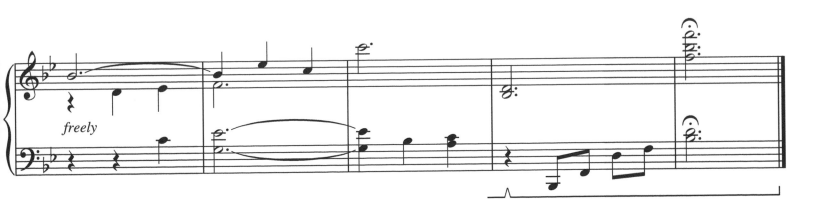

freely

IT IS WELL WITH MY SOUL

Words by HORATIO G. SPAFFORD
Music by PHILIP P. BLISS
Arranged by John Purifoy

Peacefully, with freedom

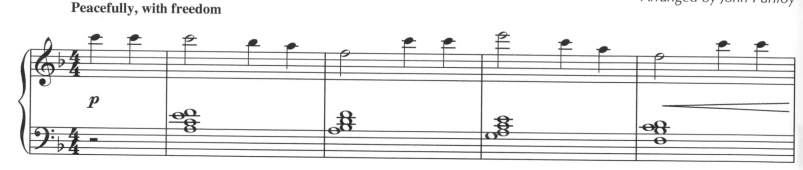

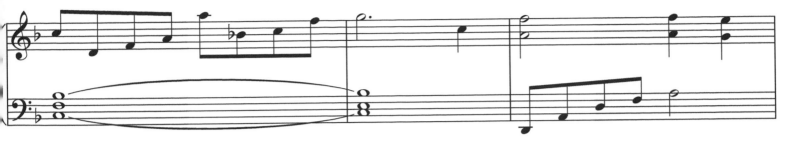

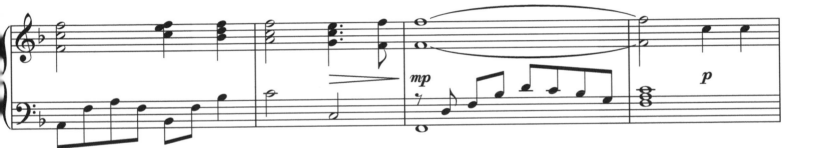

LIKE A RIVER GLORIOUS

Words by FRANCES R. HAVERGAL
Music by JAMES MOUNTAIN
Arranged by John Purifoy

Flowing, like a gentle river

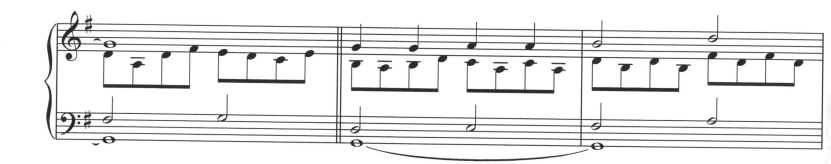

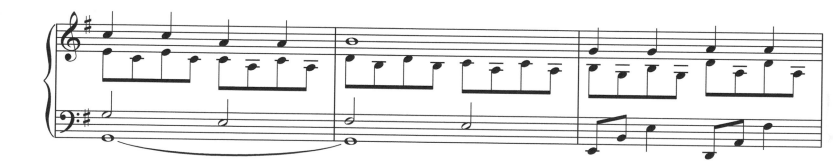

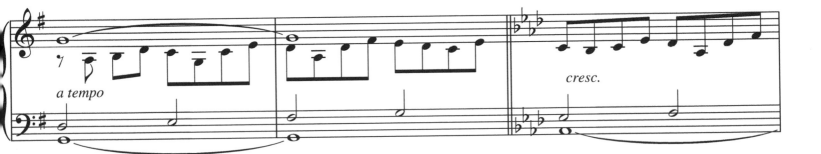

Slower, with freedom

ROCK OF AGES

Words by AUGUSTUS M. TOPLADY
V.1,2,4 altered by THOMAS COTTERILL
Music by THOMAS HASTINGS
Arranged by John Purifoy

Tempo I

molto rit.

The Best Sacred Collections for Piano

Blended Worship Piano Collection

Songs include: Amazing Grace (My Chains Are Gone) • Be Thou My Vision • I Will Rise • Joyful, Joyful, We Adore Thee • Lamb of God • Majesty • Open the Eyes of My Heart • Praise to the Lord, the Almighty • Shout to the Lord • 10,000 Reasons (Bless the Lord) • Worthy Is the Lamb • Your Name • and more.
00293528 Piano Solo $17.99

Hymn Anthology

A beautiful collection of 60 hymns arranged for piano solo, including: Abide with Me • Be Thou My Vision • Come, Thou Fount of Every Blessing • Doxology • For the Beauty of the Earth • God of Grace and God of Glory • Holy, Holy, Holy • It Is Well with My Soul • Joyful, Joyful, We Adore Thee • Let Us Break Bread Together • A Mighty Fortress Is Our God • O God, Our Help in Ages Past • Savior, like a Shepherd Lead Us • To God Be the Glory • What a Friend We Have in Jesus • and more.
00251244 Piano Solo $16.99

The Hymn Collection
arranged by Phillip Keveren

17 beloved hymns expertly and beautifully arranged for solo piano by Phillip Keveren. Includes: All Hail the Power of Jesus' Name • I Love to Tell the Story • I Surrender All • I've Got Peace Like a River • Were You There? • and more.
00311071 Piano Solo $14.99

Hymn Duets
arranged by Phillip Keveren

Includes lovely duet arrangements of: All Creatures of Our God and King • I Surrender All • It Is Well with My Soul • O Sacred Head, Now Wounded • Praise to the Lord, The Almighty • Rejoice, The Lord Is King • and more.
00311544 Piano Duet................................$14.99

Hymn Medleys
arranged by Phillip Keveren

Great medleys resonate with the human spirit, as do the truths in these moving hymns. Here Phillip Keveren combines 24 timeless favorites into eight lovely medleys for solo piano.
00311349 Piano Solo $14.99

P/V/G = Piano/Vocal/Guitar arrangements.

Prices, contents and availability subject to change without notice.

Hymns for Two
arranged by Carol Klose

12 piano duet arrangements of favorite hymns: Amazing Grace • Be Thou My Vision • Crown Him with Many Crowns • Fairest Lord Jesus • Holy, Holy, Holy • I Need Thee Every Hour • O Worship the King • What a Friend We Have in Jesus • and more.
00290544 Piano Duet.................................$12.99

It Is Well
10 BELOVED HYMNS FOR MEMORIAL SERVICES
arr. John Purifoy

10 peaceful, soul-stirring hymn settings appropriate for memorial services and general worship use. Titles include: Abide with Me • Amazing Grace • Be Still My Soul • For All the Saints • His Eye Is on the Sparrow • In the Garden • It Is Well with My Soul • Like a River Glorious • Rock of Ages • What a Friend We Have in Jesus.
00118920 Piano Solo $12.99

Ragtime Gospel Classics
arr. Steven K. Tedesco

A dozen old-time gospel favorites: Because He Lives • Goodbye World Goodbye • He Touched Me • I Saw the Light • I'll Fly Away • Keep on the Firing Line • Mansion over the Hilltop • No One Ever Cared for Me like Jesus • There Will Be Peace in the Valley for Me • Victory in Jesus • What a Day That Will Be • Where Could I Go.
00142449 Piano Solo $11.99

Ragtime Gospel Hymns
arranged by Steven Tedesco

15 traditional gospel hymns, including: At Calvary • Footsteps of Jesus • Just a Closer Walk with Thee • Leaning on the Everlasting Arms • What a Friend We Have in Jesus • When We All Get to Heaven • and more.
00311763 Piano Solo $10.99

Sacred Classics for Solo Piano
arr. John Purifoy

10 timeless songs of faith, masterfully arranged by John Purifoy. Because He Lives • Easter Song • Glorify Thy Name • Here Am I, Send Me • I'd Rather Have Jesus • Majesty • On Eagle's Wings • There's Something About That Name • We Shall Behold Him • Worthy Is the Lamb.
00141703 Piano Solo $14.99

Raise Your Hands
PIANO SOLOS FOR BLENDED WORSHIP
arr. Heather Sorenson

10 uplifting and worshipful solos crafted by Heather Sorenson. Come Thou Fount, Come Thou King • God of Heaven • Holy Is the Lord (with "Holy, Holy, Holy") • Holy Spirit • I Will Rise • In Christ Alone • Raise Your Hands • Revelation Song • 10,000 Reasons (Bless the Lord) • Your Name (with "All Hail the Power of Jesus' Name").
00231579 Piano Solo $14.99

Seasonal Sunday Solos for Piano

24 blended selections grouped by occasion. Includes: Breath of Heaven (Mary's Song) • Come, Ye Thankful People, Come • Do You Hear What I Hear • God of Our Fathers • In the Name of the Lord • Mary, Did You Know? • Mighty to Save • Spirit of the Living God • The Wonderful Cross • and more.
00311971 Piano Solo $16.99

Sunday Solos for Piano

30 blended selections, perfect for the church pianist. Songs include: All Hail the Power of Jesus' Name • Be Thou My Vision • Great Is the Lord • Here I Am to Worship • Majesty • Open the Eyes of My Heart • and many more.
00311272 Piano Solo $17.99

More Sunday Solos for Piano

A follow-up to *Sunday Solos for Piano*, this collection features 30 more blended selections perfect for the church pianist. Includes: Agnus Dei • Come, Thou Fount of Every Blessing • The Heart of Worship • How Great Thou Art • Immortal, Invisible • O Worship the King • Shout to the Lord • Thy Word • We Fall Down • and more.
00311864 Piano Solo $16.99

Even More Sunday Solos for Piano

30 blended selections, including: Ancient Words • Brethren, We Have Met to Worship • How Great Is Our God • Lead On, O King Eternal • Offering • Savior, Like a Shepherd Lead Us • We Bow Down • Worthy of Worship • and more.
00312098 Piano Solo $16.99